how to draw
cartoons

igloo

how to draw cartoons

contents

introduction

Cartooning is a great hobby – you can do it anytime, anywhere, and you'll only need a few pieces of inexpensive equipment to get started. Whether you're a complete beginner or a budding artist, this book is for you.

In the first section, you'll learn the basic principles of drawing and construction. This is followed by a series of projects, ranging from the simplest line drawings, through superheroes and manga characters, to the most complex fantasy creatures. But however tricky the illustration may appear, you'll find it easy to re-create using the simple step-by-step guides.

Once you've mastered these skills, it's over to you to start creating characters of your own – so get cartooning now!

how to draw **cartoons**

You don't need lots of expensive equipment to start cartooning. Here's a list of the basic materials.

Paper, and lots of it. Plain photocopy or laser printer paper is inexpensive and has a smooth surface, so it's easy to erase your mistakes. Scrap paper is useful when you're experimenting, and a small sketch pad comes in handy if you see something interesting when you're out and about.

Pencils – soft and hard. Softer pencils are good for sketching and shading, and are easy to erase. Harder pencils have a sharper point, so you can use them for the finer details. You'll need a good eraser and a pencil sharpener, too.

A small ruler is useful and you might want to buy a stencil for drawing circles and ovals. (Otherwise you can draw around something like a cup or bottle cap for a perfect circle.)

You will need a waterproof black pen to ink over your pencil drawings. These come in varying thicknesses, so you could get a selection.

Finally, for coloring your finished artwork, you will need some colored pencils, felt pens, or paints and paintbrushes.

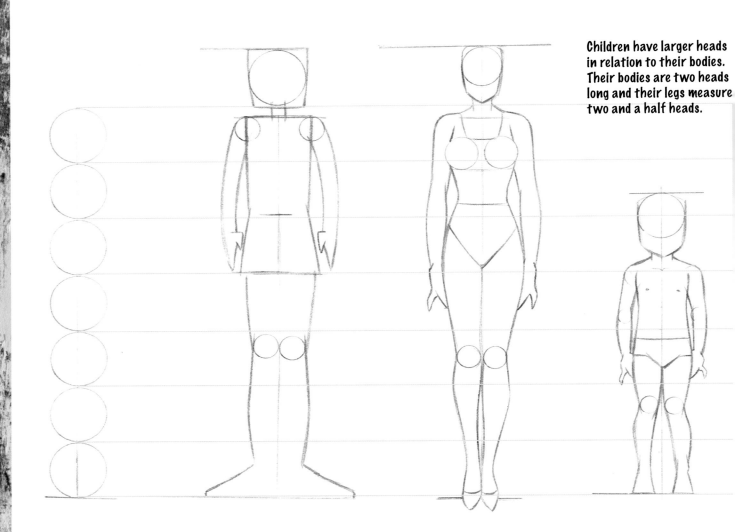

Children have larger heads in relation to their bodies. Their bodies are two heads long and their legs measure two and a half heads.

If you measure an person's head from the crown to the chin, you can work out the proportions of the body. The adult torso is the equivalent of three heads and the legs are four heads long.

Human proportions

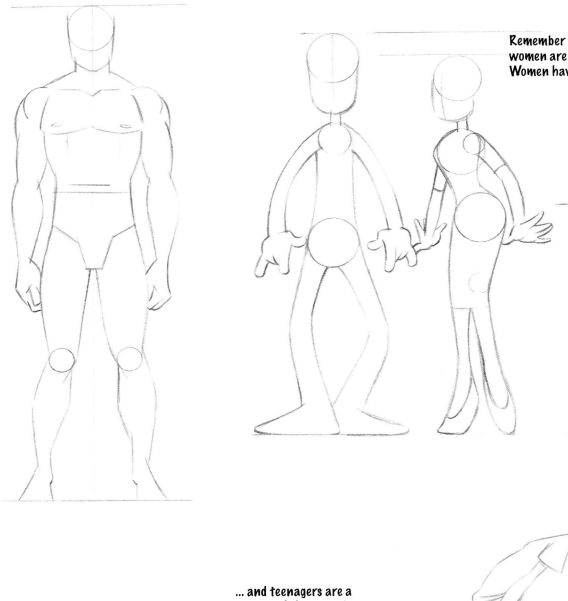

Remember that men and women are different shapes. Women have curves!

... and teenagers are a species of their own!

Once you've mastered the basics, it's time to bring your figures to life. Try making simple sketches of people in different positions to build up a library of useful material.

It's a good idea to carry a pencil and paper at all times, so you can do a quick sketch if you spot someone doing something interesting.

Body language

Sketches don't have to show detail, you just need to capture the movement.

The eyes are one of the main features that show how a character is feeling.

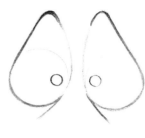
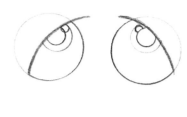
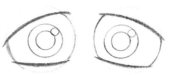

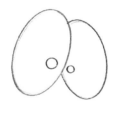

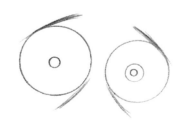

Try combining different mouths and eyes to see how many expressions you can create.

Eyes, noses, and mouths

Noses come in all shapes and sizes.

Mouths are as important as eyes when it comes to expressing emotion.

how to draw **cartoons**

Draw a page of circles and try out some of these facial expressions.

To express surprise, the eyes should be wide with small central pupils. Eyebrows are raised and the mouth can be lower, as if the jaw is hitting the ground.

An angry face has eyebrows that turn down in the middle and almost meet. The pupils are small and close together and the eyes are narrowed. The mouth is straight or turned down.

A sad face has downturned eyebrows, the pupil is at the top of the eyeball and the mouth turns down at the corners

A happy face has wide open eyes, raised eyebrows, and an open, smiling mouth, showing lots of teeth.

There's no place for subtlety in cartooning. Cartoon faces usually show greatly exaggerated emotions.

Facial expressions

Faces can add animation to anything. In the world of cartooning all sorts of things can have a face!

how to draw **cartoons**

Have a go at drawing these crazy creatures. They are all based on very simple shapes. Always draw in pencil first, so you can erase any mistakes. Once you are happy with your drawing, you can go over the lines with a black pen.

Try the simple shading techniques shown here to make your drawings more 3-D.

Now try drawing the more realistic animals on these pages, following the simple step-by-step guides.

how to draw **cartoons**

Many animals are based on a combination of circles and ovals. When you have mastered the creatures on these pages, see how many others you can draw using the same principles.

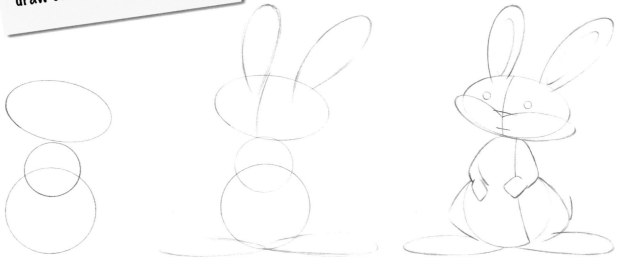

how to draw **cartoons**

Modern American style cartoons are all about extreme body shapes and extreme situations. Body proportions are often off the scale and don't always follow the rules set out earlier in this book.

1 Bodies are a series of shapes put together to form a human being. Start with a circle or cone for the head. Dad always has a huge waist from sitting around too much.

2 Large feet and arms that start lower down the body give him that slumped couch potato look.

Run a vertical line down where you want the center of the face to be. Then add a horizontal line across the face to find the eyeline.

The eyes are circles and should be centered on the line. The tops of the ears should just touch it.

The nose sits on the vertical line just below the eyes.

The lower the mouth is between the bottom of his nose and his chin, the more stupid he appears.

Receding hair and glasses make a character look older. A wide round face with the features clustered in the center makes him look younger.

③

Now it's time to fill in the details.

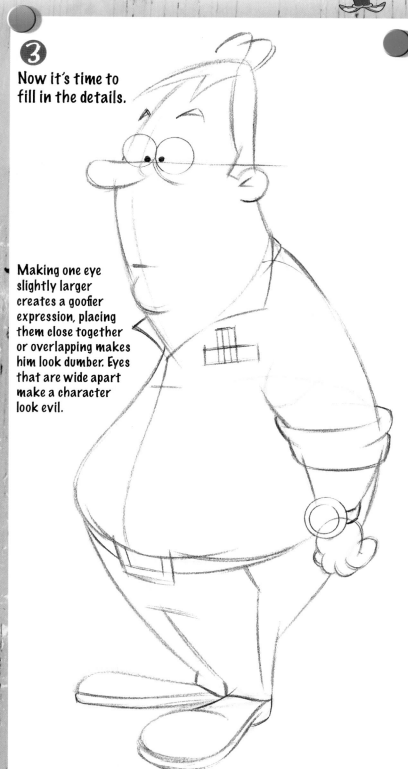

Making one eye slightly larger creates a goofier expression, placing them close together or overlapping makes him look dumber. Eyes that are wide apart make a character look evil.

4

When you are happy with your drawing, ink over the lines using a black pen, then erase the pencil marks.

5

Now color your drawing. This character is flat-colored without any shading or highlights, but the shadow behind his back makes him look more three-dimensional.

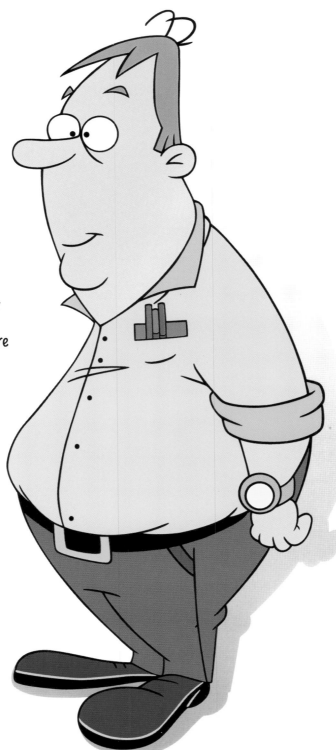

how to draw **cartoons**

1

Draw the two aliens in pencil, following these simple steps. If you want to illustrate them side by side, as shown overleaf, make sure you position them correctly from the start.

There's no need to stick to the normal rules of bodily proportions when your character's an extra-terrestrial!

2

When you are happy with
your drawing, ink over the
lines using a black pen, then
erase the pencil marks.

Sci-fi style

③ Now color your drawing. Extra-terrestrials can be any color you like – the crazier the better. Note the simple shading on these two characters, which makes them appear more 3-D.

Don't forget the shadows on the ground beneath the figures.

how to draw **cartoons**

These spacecraft are based on simple shapes. If you want to draw them on a background as shown on the following pages, make sure you position them in the right place from the start.

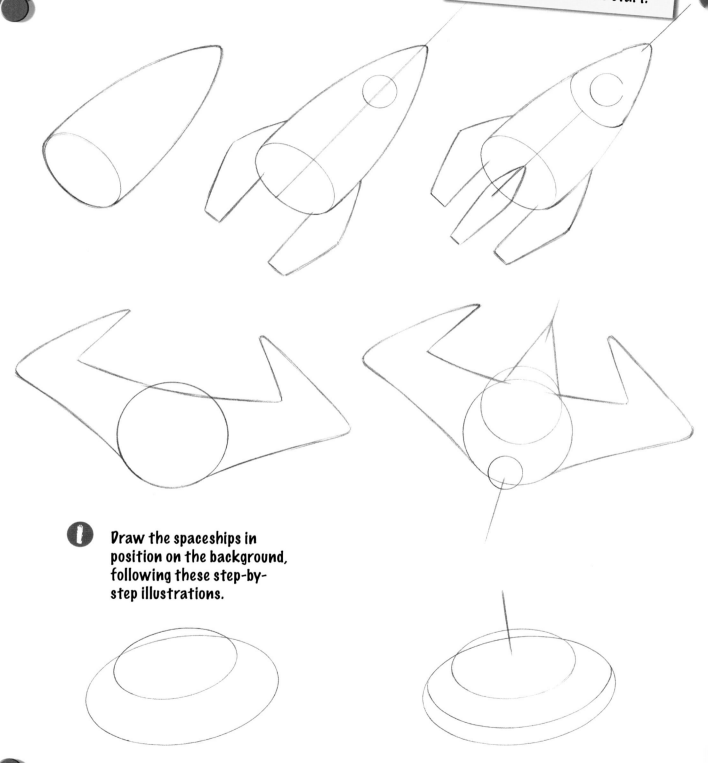

1 Draw the spaceships in position on the background, following these step-by-step illustrations.

Sci-fi style

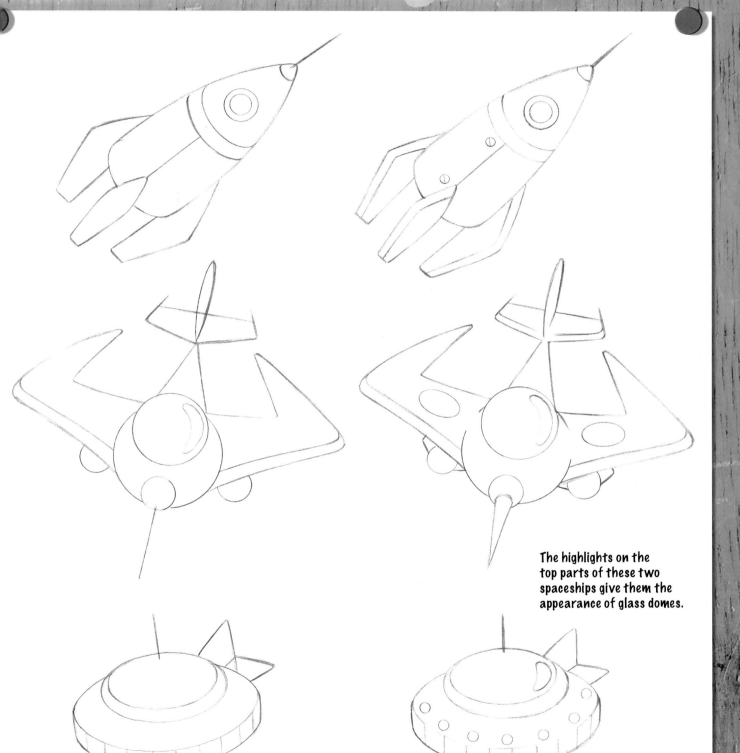

The highlights on the top parts of these two spaceships give them the appearance of glass domes.

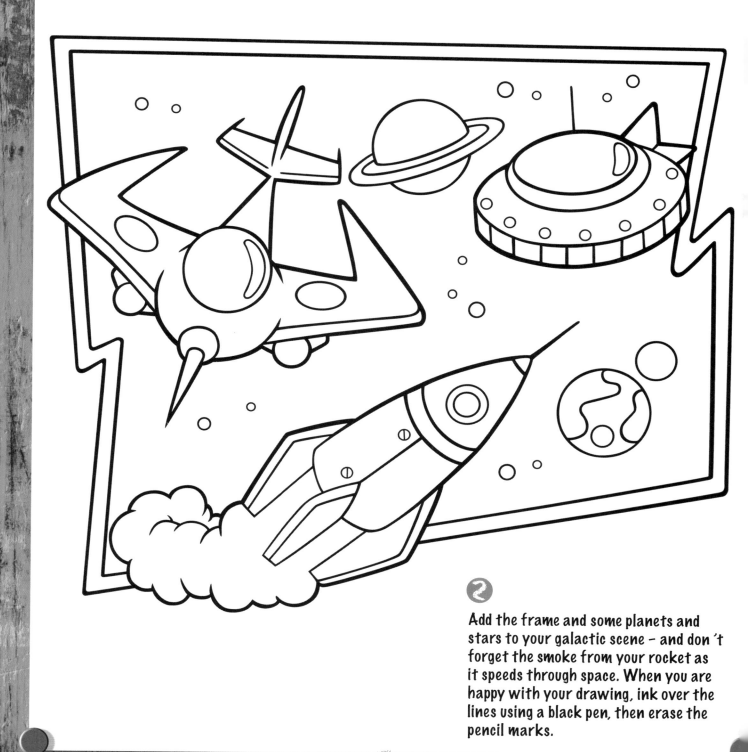

2

Add the frame and some planets and stars to your galactic scene – and don´t forget the smoke from your rocket as it speeds through space. When you are happy with your drawing, ink over the lines using a black pen, then erase the pencil marks.

Sci-fi style

3

Now color your drawing. Note how some parts of the spacecraft are a lighter tone and others are darker, giving a 3-D effect. The stars and planets have lighter rings around them, so they look as if they are glowing.

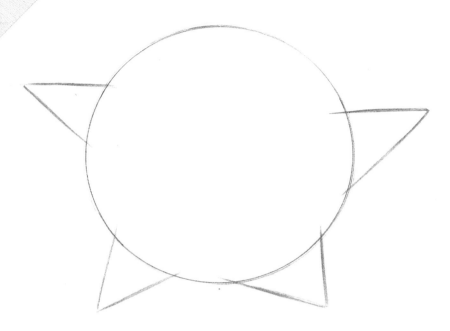

1

Begin by drawing a circle in the middle of the page. Add two triangles for the arms and two for the legs.

2

Draw a vertical line down the middle, so you can position the features – this strange creature has rectangular eyes. Then sketch in the hands and feet and add a bow on top of the head.

Small triangles around the outside of the circle give the character a spiky appearance.

3

Now add details to the features, such as the eyelashes, cheeks, and tongue.

When you are happy with
your drawing, go over the
lines with a black pen, then
erase the pencil marks.

 5

Now color your manga creature. You can use a single color for the whole body, or a lighter shade at the top, getting darker towards the bottom, as shown here. Don't forget the shadow on the ground beneath the character.

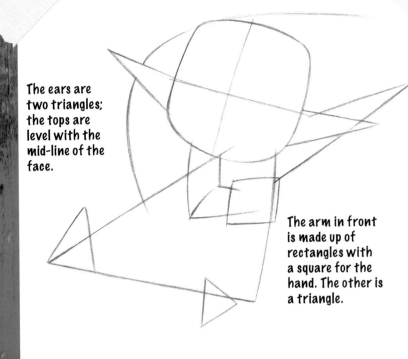

The ears are two triangles; the tops are level with the mid-line of the face.

The arm in front is made up of rectangles with a square for the hand. The other is a triangle.

Manga characters usually have spiky hair, large round eyes, and small noses.

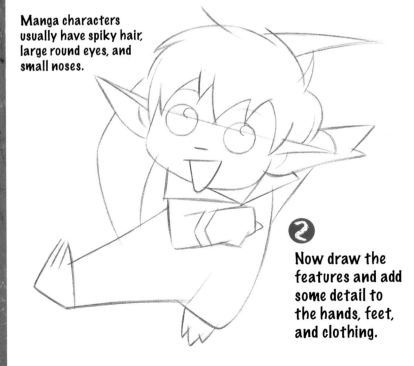

This character's head is square with rounded corners. Draw a cross through the middle, so you can position the features. The body and feet are triangles and the tail arches from the middle of the body over the top of the head.

② Now draw the features and add some detail to the hands, feet, and clothing.

Experiment with different mouth shapes. Manga characters normally have small mouths unless they are laughing, then the mouth takes over most of the face, exaggerating the emotion.

Large eyes are a feature of manga-style illustration and are used to express emotion. This is usually taken to extremes, so if a character is crying, tears pour out by the bucketload. Female characters normally have eyelashes, while male characters don't.

③

Complete your drawing, rounding off the hands and feet and adding more detail to the ears, hair, tail, and clothing.

4

When you are happy with your drawing, ink over the lines using a black pen, then erase the pencil marks.

5

Now color your character. Use a lighter tone for the highlights and darker shades for the shadows.

Manga characters often have brightly-colored hair.

Add a shadow on the ground beneath the figure.

how to draw **cartoons**

1

Start with three lines, showing the center of the body, the outstretched arm, and the front leg, then flesh out your character, using circles and sausage shapes.

Classic retro style

The eyes often amount to little more than a black dot surrounded by simple lines. Eyebrows are important in illustrating expressions.

2 Now add the facial features and the clothes and shoes.

To show a character running, try shading an oval shape beneath each foot. This gives the impression of someone in mid-flight.

3

Add the details to the
clothing. When you are
happy with your drawing,
ink over the lines using a
black pen, then erase the
pencil marks.

4

Now color your drawing. This character has been colored using very simple shading along his back, the backs of his arms and legs, and around the edges of his face and hands.

how to draw **cartoons**

Vehicles are often based around rectangles and squares, but this streamlined speedster is mainly made up of circular and oval shapes.

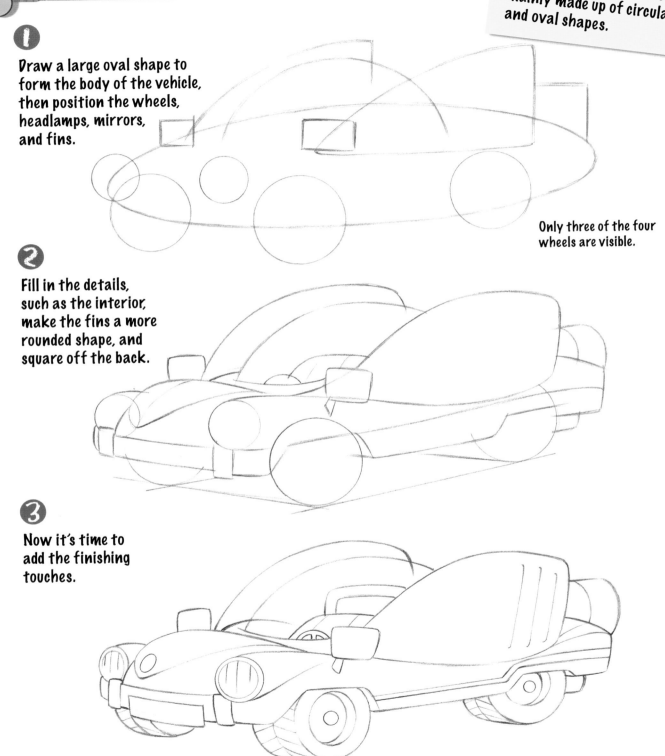

1 Draw a large oval shape to form the body of the vehicle, then position the wheels, headlamps, mirrors, and fins.

Only three of the four wheels are visible.

2 Fill in the details, such as the interior, make the fins a more rounded shape, and square off the back.

3 Now it's time to add the finishing touches.

4

When you are happy with your drawing, ink over the lines using a black pen, then erase the pencil marks.

5

Now color your drawing. This vehicle has been flat-colored, without any shading.

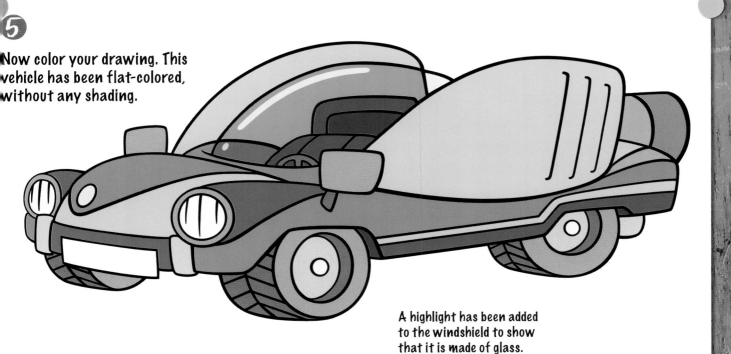

A highlight has been added to the windshield to show that it is made of glass.

1 A typical superhero has a prominent chest with a narrow waist and hips. Men always have a very defined jawline – square and manly.

A superhero's cape flies in the breeze (even when he's standing still), but he never has a hair out of place.

3 A jutting jaw, with a cleft in the chin, and furrowed brows will give your character the classic superhero expression.

2 Male characters have more muscles than the average guy, but beware of making your superhero look like a balloon man.

4 When you are happy with your drawing, ink over the lines using a black pen, then erase the pencil marks.

5 Now color your drawing. This character has been flat-colored, without any shading.

1

Female superheroes have a slim, athletic build. They don't have defined muscles like their male counterparts.

They are usually very attractive, but their faces are strong and angular, rather than soft and pretty.

② When your pencil drawing is complete, go over the lines with a black pen and erase all the pencil marks.

③ Now color your drawing. This illustration has been flat-colored, without any shading.

1 First draw the basic outline of your character.

2 Sketch in horizontal and vertical lines to mark the center of the face and of the body.

3 Now add the details to the features, hands, and clothing.

Unlike the hands of most of the classic cartoon animals, human characters' hands have four fingers and one thumb.

The faces of classic cartoon characters follow all the norma rules – the eyes are one eye width apart and are positioned halfway down the head, the nose and ears are just below the midline of the face, and the mouth is halfway between the nose and the chin.

4

Complete your illustration by drawing the fishing line, and the gnome's glasses and belt buckle.

5

When your pencil drawing is finished, go over the lines with a black pen and erase all the pencil marks.

6

Now color your drawing. This illustration has quite complex shading and highlights.

1 Although this cute creature is dressed in human clothes, it doesn't follow the normal rules of human proportions.

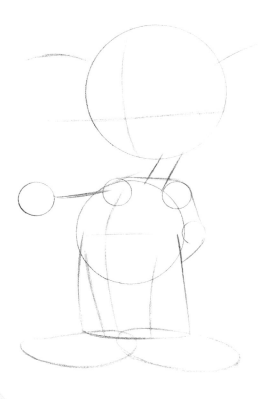

2 The large eyes reach from below the center of the face almost to the top of the head.

Classic cartoon animals usually have three fingers and one thumb. Their hands are very simple, without details such as knuckles.

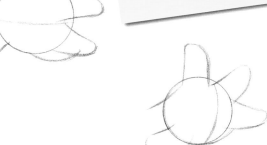

3 Add the details to the nightshirt and bows, and give your character some eyelashes.

4 When your pencil drawing is complete, go over the lines with a black pen and erase all the pencil marks.

5 Now color your drawing. This illustration has subtle shading and highlights. Using brown, rather than black, for outlining the animal's fur, as shown here, gives a softer appearance.

how to draw **cartoons**

1 This character's body is covered by his flowing robes, so initially it is just drawn as a triangle, but make sure that the bodily proportions are still correct.

The wizard is facing toward the left, so the line down the middle of his face and body should be to the left of center.

The hands are drawn as boxes to begin with, then more detail is added, as shown below.

2 Now add the features and a long beard.

Drawing hands can be tricky, but it's a skill worth mastering as gestures add expression to your character.

Unlike most cartoon characters, who usually have sausage-like fingers, the wizard's hands are more realistic, so take note of the difference in length between the fingers and thumb.

③ Now add some folds to the robes and more detail to the features.

Don't forget a sprinkle of magic!

4

Once you are happy with your drawing, go over the lines with a black pen and erase the pencil marks. Color the wizard, giving him a magical glow.

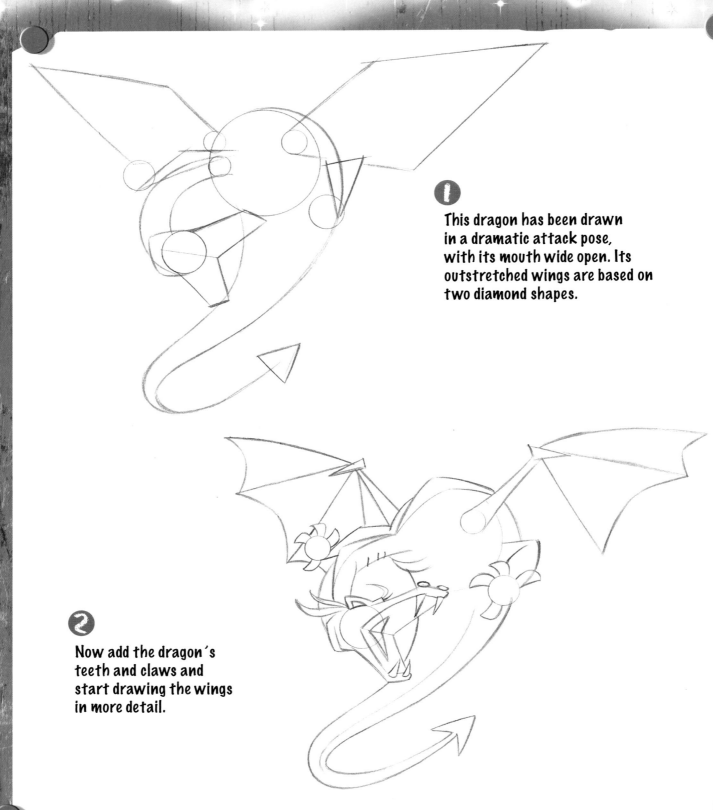

1 This dragon has been drawn in a dramatic attack pose, with its mouth wide open. Its outstretched wings are based on two diamond shapes.

2 Now add the dragon's teeth and claws and start drawing the wings in more detail.

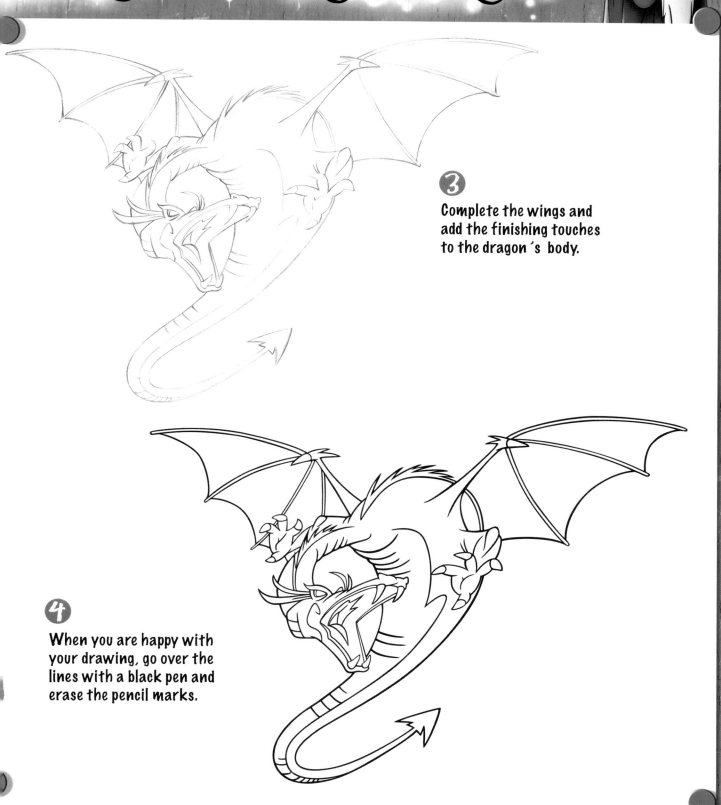

3 Complete the wings and add the finishing touches to the dragon´s body.

4 When you are happy with your drawing, go over the lines with a black pen and erase the pencil marks.

5

Now color your drawing. Here the use of shading and highlights really brings the dragon to life. It looks as if it's about to leap out from the page.